FIRE YOUR BOSS

HOW TO QUIT YOUR JOB, STOP SELLING
YOUR TIME AND START MAKING PASSIVE
INCOME WHILE YOU SLEEP…AND POSSIBLY
MOVE TO A TROPICAL ISLAND

JONATHAN GREEN

Edited by
ALICE FOGLIATA

Paperback ISBN 13: 978-1730981029

Hardback ISBN 13: 978-1947667181

Hardback ISBN 10: 1947667181

CONTENTS

•

FREE GIFT

How do you know the exact moment when you're ready to fire your boss and say goodbye to the cubicle life forever?

I have an AWESOME checklist for you.

To get the Quit My Job checklist, just click this link right inside your Kindle:

https://ServeNoMaster.com/fire

A NOTE ABOUT LINKS

Throughout this book, I mention other books, images, links, and additional content. All of that can be found at:

ServeNoMaster.com/FireYourBoss

You don't have to worry about trying to remember any other links or the names of anything mentioned in this book. Just enjoy the journey and focus on taking control of your destiny.

PART I

YOUR TICKET TO FREEDOM

INTRODUCTION

W hen I was fifteen years old, my junior varsity soccer coach shattered my self-esteem with a hammer. At that fragile young age, I did not yet know what I was capable of, so when he told me that I wasn't good enough, I believed him.

Like many American kids in the era of the video game, I grew up an inside kid, watching television and playing video games for hours. As a natural athlete, my father did his best to get me out into the world. I played many sports from baseball to soccer to basketball. I dabbled a little bit in everything, but the only sport that stuck was soccer.

When I started high school and discovered that sports were mandatory, I chose to play soccer. As nearly the slowest person on the team, I naturally decided to learn to be a goalie.

As a freshman, I was the backup goalie. My job revolved around supporting the junior varsity starter. I made sure he was warmed up before games, kept him warm during half-time when it was cold out, and helped him in any other way he might need. We weren't great friends, but at least he didn't hate me like the first-string goalie for the Varsity team.

One day, a miracle happened. The first-string goalie broke his wrist in the middle of the game. I couldn't believe it. I thought, "Surely, he's going to be fine. There's no way Coach would ever put me in." Luckily for me, he had no choice. Despite his utter lack of faith in me, he put me in, I saved the game, and we won. Best of all, my dad was there to see my victory.

Suddenly, the sun was rising on the Nation of Jonathan. The poor injured kid was out for the season, but I couldn't have been more excited. I was sure I would get to be the goalie for the rest of the season and prove myself to the other players and, more importantly, to my father.

The next Monday at practice, the junior varsity coach picked the tallest guy and said, "You're the new goalie." I was devastated. I had been training the whole season. Why wouldn't he put me in the game?

He said to me something I'll never forget. "Doug's taller than you. He'll be a better goalie."

This wasn't the first and certainly not the last time I encountered such a simplistic mindset. I have a feeling that you've encountered the same kinds of things in your life, where there was someone out there who wouldn't give you a shot. This was just the beginning of my soccer odyssey. I'll share the story of the rest of that season with you before we finish this book. But for now, it's time to talk about you.

There's a very good chance that, if you were just given the right opportunities, if someone would just give you a shot, you could do something amazing. Unfortunately, we spend so much of our lives waiting for someone else to give us a shot, waiting for someone else to say, "Hey, I'm putting you in." That's all I wanted to hear from my coach. "Jonathan, get out there. I'm going to give you a shot."

You've picked up this book, and you've begun your journey with me. This is your shot. Until now, maybe no one else has seen your potential, but I do. I know what it's like to have no one in your corner.

It's time to stop waiting for someone else to give you a shot; it's time to start creating your own opportunities.

UNLOCK YOUR SUPERPOWER

No matter where you are in life, you need a backup plan. Regardless of your career, how much money you have, or how much debt you're in, you need a plan B.

If there's one thing I learned from my soccer coach shattering my self-esteem, it's that you cannot rely on other people to give you the life you want. We're all born with certain advantages and disadvantages, but it's what we do with those that matter.

Being born with more opportunities doesn't always mean your life will be better. When's the last time you heard of someone who was born to a trust fund accomplishing anything significant with their lives? People born into wealth and lives of ease have a lack of need, which means they don't feel the drive to accomplish anything.

On the other hand, far too many Americans are waiting for that next raise to get ahead. For any of us, as our salary increases, so does our debt.

The average American spends 10 percent more than they make.[1] If you're making $1,000 a month, you increase your debt every month by $100. If you're making $10,000 a month, your debt increases by $1,000. That's why so many people go from having amazing houses and beautiful cars to living in studio apartments or worse.

We're a nation that doesn't plan for the future, and it's time to change.

In this book, we're going to go on a short and powerful journey together, discussing different business models and ways you can start to build your plan B. Whether you're working, in between jobs, or afraid you're going to lose your job, these are business models that you can start implementing today to create a bulwark between you and the loss of your primary revenue stream.

This is the core tenet of my belief system and everything I teach at Serve No Master. If you learn one thing from this book, it's that you should always have multiple revenue streams. As soon as you build one business model, you should start on the next one.

Many young entrepreneurs find success through luck. The first thing they try works, which is fantastic, but then they quit their old job. They're back to a single revenue stream, and they're back to being vulnerable. As soon as something goes wrong, and there's a hiccup or a shift in the market, they're suddenly back to zero revenue streams.

I hope that the first thing you try with me works. However, what I want is for us to build out a plan B, a plan C, and a plan D.

Every business model we're going to discuss in this book can work cooperatively with the other models to provide you with multiple revenue streams and inputs into your business.

An online business can be broken down into three pieces – traffic, experience, and sales. Someone visits your website for the first time (traffic). They read a blog post or some of your emails (experience). They feel they know you well enough to purchase from you (sales). As we go deeper into this process, this simple three-step business model will allow you to make money even while you sleep – the ultimate superpower.

I implore you to go along with me on this journey. Allow me to show you what's possible and how much you can transform your life with just a couple hours a week.

WHY IS THIS BOOK FREE?

Y ou may be wondering, "If the information in this book is so useful, why is Jonathan giving it away for free?"

That's a good question.

My primary book, *Serve No Master*, has been on the top of the business charts since 2016. That book is not free, and it never will be. However, by charging for that book, I realized that I'm leaving a lot of people behind.

There are plenty of people who can't afford a $10 book. Whether it's a lack of faith, trust, self-confidence, or funds, there's something holding people back from making that first decision and buying my book.

I want to be able to reach and help as many people as possible. I want to get my message out there and create opportunities for people who are just starting and who aren't ready to grab a book by an author they've never heard of.

I'm not famous. I don't run a Fortune 500 company. I didn't sell my business to a social media platform after eighteen months. I'm just an independent author who lives on a tropical island. I made my dreams come true, and I want to teach you how to do the same.

There are two ways that you can influence the world. The first is to influence a small number of people significantly. This is what happens when you adopt a child. You spend a lot of one-on-one time with them, and you transform their life.

When you do one-on-one coaching or mentoring, it takes a considerable amount of your time, but the impact is significant.

At the other end of the influence spectrum, you reach a significant number of people but affect them only a small amount. This is the type of impact a motivational speaker has. They give a speech to a room full of people, teaching them how to improve their self-esteem and take on the world. They may not work with each audience member one-on-one, but they certainly give a lot of people the self-confidence they need to move on to the next step and achieve something great.

I've impacted many people by working with them one-on-one, but I want to broaden my reach and connect with more people. That's why I've created a book that's available to everyone. I want to increase my influence.

If, at the end of this book, the only thing you've learned is that it's possible to improve your life, then my mission is accomplished. It doesn't matter if you choose to follow me after this book, or if you find someone else that better fits your skill set and the goals you want to accomplish. I have already affected you enough to give you the hope to get to that next step.

4

BUILDING RUNWAY

I f you're like the majority of the people who read my books, you already have a full-time job that takes up so much of your day that you have very little time left to invest in building your own business. You certainly can't dedicate huge amounts of time to a business that won't show returns for six to twelve months.

That's why we start by focusing on building runway, which is where you generate revenue fast.

There are two ways to make money with an online business. The first is by selling your time; the second is by generating passive income.

Most of us approach life only using the first method. We trade our time for money. We spend our time in an office, and we get paid for it.

Whether you work for someone else or for yourself, this is the first phase of your entrepreneurial journey. This is how I started, and it's how everyone starts. Selling time is the best way to build runway.

Whenever I want to fund a new project, I sell some time. When I want to put out a new product, but I don't quite have enough funds to do it, I spend some time ghostwriting for someone else, and they give me the funds I need to begin creating my product.

It's critical to understand how this process works. Making enough money to quit your job is not the end of this journey; it's merely the end of phase one. When the first revenue stream you build is strong enough to allow you to leave your job, you have more control over your schedule, but you still have a single point of failure.

My journey began when I lost my job teaching at one of the best universities in the United States. I was fired in dramatic fashion, which I recount in great detail in *Serve No Master*.

After losing that job, I realized I never wanted to go back under someone else's power. I never wanted to be in a position where someone else could fire me ever again. I had an incredibly limited savings account and built my runway in the worst way possible – using a credit card.

I started out by selling local services to small businesses, helping them enter the twenty-first century. I improved their websites, got them traffic, and helped them turn their websites into actual profit-generating tools. This required me to meet with my clients face-to-face.

I would drive all over town from coffee shop to coffee shop, from Panera to Starbucks. How many paninis and hot chocolates could I choke down in a single day? It felt like I was on an odyssey to find out the answer to that question.

When I finally had enough revenue that I was no longer afraid of losing my home and going hungry, I began to move into phase two, the passive income stream where I make money while I sleep.

There's nothing I love more than waking up to emails alerting me that sales have come in. I have enough books on

Amazon and enough products out in the world that I will always generate revenue while I sleep. This is exactly what I want for you.

The first step in this process is to work together to build your runway. Once that's established, we're going to develop passive income streams.

If you're working nine to five for someone else right now, that's a very long day. It's hard to come home after all those hours and put in another eight-hour shift on your new business. I know what that's like. I have three kids who need a lot of attention.

We're going to work on eliminating that day job. We're going to generate enough revenue selling your time for more than you're currently getting paid to allow you to fire your boss and leave that job behind.

Whatever your boss is paying you right now is less than you're worth. If your boss is paying you $10 an hour, I guarantee you you're worth more. Companies would go out of business if they paid employees what they are worth.

By having a plan B in place, you're not going to be financially devastated if your other revenue streams disappear. Building runway prepares you to build passive revenue streams and protects you if the worst should happen and you lost your job for reasons outside your control.

Let's go on this journey together. Let's start building runway and begin establishing passive revenue streams so that you have a financial legacy.

5

BREAKING THE MONEY-TO-TIME LINK

Right now, you're stuck in phase zero. This is where you work for someone else, get paid a fixed amount of money for each hour or week you work and have no control over your destiny.

It's time to launch into phase one. As we start building your runway, you will soon realize that your time is worth far more than you ever thought.

Despite the feeling of freedom that comes with phase one, the process is not complete until you break the chain that ties you to time. Whether you're a consultant, selling your services, or working on any of the business models I'll be sharing with you later in this book, you're still tying money to time.

Once your runway is built, however, it's time to take flight and enter the second phase of your career – the passive revenue stream. This is where you make money for the same work multiple times.

Even when I was performing services for other businesses, I always approached a project with the goal of making money three times on that single service.

I would first use the money from one client to buy software and training that I needed to service them. Then, I would use that software and training to service other clients and generate a second stream of revenue from that first investment. To produce the third revenue stream, I would use that training or those tools on my own business.

If you approach every online business opportunity with the goal of getting paid three times, you will increase your efficiency, and you'll cut the time-to-money connection faster. The faster you cut that connection, the sooner you'll be free.

Let me paint you a picture of what freedom looks like. I dictated this book on a beach that's only thirty minutes away from my house. (I have a beach in my front yard, but it's not quiet enough to dictate.) I walked along the beach in about an inch of water under some palm trees in the middle of paradise while my wife and son played about twenty yards away from me.

Freedom isn't so bad.

What's even more amazing is that I only have to dictate this book once, and I can give it away an infinite amount of times. I'm never going to charge money for this particular book, but every other book that I do charge for follows the same process. I write it once, and I sell it tens of thousands of times.

I see the Internet as the great equalizer. It doesn't matter where you're from or what your situation is. The playing field is even thanks to the Internet. Anyone can learn how to build a business online with minimal investment.

As you're approaching this process, I want you to focus on getting to phase two. Some people get stuck in phase one, and they are very successful, but they're trapped.

An example of a phase one business is a family that

opens a corner convenience shop and works twelve hours a day, seven days a week. There's always a member of their family behind the counter. They can generate huge amounts of money, but they're always there.

During phase one, it's easy to paint yourself into a corner. You can build a business that's pure service and requires your continual time. Before you realize it, you're stuck.

When I founded Serve No Master, my idea was to build a business around something other than my personality. A business built around Jonathan Green as a brand is unsellable. It's not like the Dread Pirate Roberts from *The Princess Bride*. I can't retire so someone else can be the next Jonathan Green.

That's why I built a business called Serve No Master. I wanted it to have a name that was separate from my personal identity. Unfortunately, despite my best efforts, my face, my voice, and my words are everywhere. Despite our best efforts, we can end up tied to our businesses.

It can be hard to break through to phase two. I haven't broken through to phase three, which is where you sell your business and retire. That's not on my roadmap. When you want to do that, you're going to need to read a different book. Maybe even a book I write in ten years when I do sell a business!

Keep phase two in your sights. Keep the hope alive that you will be able to make or do something once and sell it multiple times. That is when you've broken the bond between time and income.

6

PLAY TO WIN

I 've never written a free, mass-market book before because people take action based on their investments. Because this book is free, many people will download it, few will start to read it, even less will finish it, and only a small number will take action.

You're far more likely to put your back into a course that cost you $10,000 than a book that you found for free in your friend's garage.

When I was twenty-seven, my roommate was so bad at relationships that someone gave him a book on how to be better at dating. Because it was free, he never read it, and he never got better at dating.

However, I saw the book on his bed stand and decided to borrow it. I read it in a single day, transformed my approach to dating, and now I'm married with three kids.

There will always be people who will take something for free but take no action. Luckily, our world is also filled with autodidacts who will grab any sort of knowledge they can get their hands on, teach themselves all that they can, and put their knowledge to good use. I want you to be one of those people.

It's easy to approach making money online like the lottery or a game. I'm fascinated by the way online gambling works. As much as there are loads of casinos where you can gamble with real money, I'm also targeted with advertising all the time for pretend casinos where you play with pretend money. I'm sure there's a reason why they do this. They probably get you in the free casino and talk you into the paid casino because they convince you that you're going to be a winner.

It is very dangerous to mingle real money with imaginary money.

And it is easy for us to mingle real money with pretend money online. We can play with pretend money and think that we'll then win real money. In the same way, if you think of what I'm teaching you as a game, you remove the risk of feeling bad if you fail. But you also remove the possibility of success.

One of the first steps I teach in every single one of my books is to start a new budget. Everything you spend comes from your business budget. If you buy a book about Space Marines, which is my favorite type of book, you don't expect a return on that investment. If you spend three bucks, you don't expect to earn the $3 back. However, if you buy a business book with the same $3, it should teach you enough to earn the money back.

Earlier this year, I hired a consultant to help me with my numbers. He went through my business, helped me analyze things and showed me where there were holes in my business. I made back triple what he cost within three days.

I saw his bill as an investment. I didn't pay him to be my buddy; I paid him to help me improve my business. He's the first consultant ever to give me advice that worked. He gave me five steps, I took his advice, and I made more money.

If you want to be successful and make it to phase two, you've got to get serious. You have to decide that you're going to play to win. If you just put your toe in the water, you'll never learn how to swim. You have to make the conscious choice to change your life.

I had been a dabbling entrepreneur for more than a decade when I got fired. I'd started businesses before, but I never really believed in them, even though they were profitable.

Only when I lost my job did I realize that I had to make it as an entrepreneur. That's when it dawned on me. My entire life, I'd always had a toe in the water. But success would never come until I took a breath and jumped in.

You have to be proactive and start acting like a business. Whether you get a tax ID or set up a separate business account, there are specific steps you should take to show the world you're serious about this. Plant your flag on the moon and say, "I'm here, this is real, and this is my business."

Make a decision that you're here to win – you're serious about changing your life, you want to accomplish great things, and you want what this book teaches to work.

This book was not created to make you feel good. If I can generate hope in you, that's awesome because hope leads to action. Hope is the first step. Hope means that you believe that there is a possibility that this will work.

CONTROL YOUR SPEND

It's time to take action and start a new budget. Everything you spend from now on comes from your business budget, and everything you spend from your business budget needs to be written down.

You have one resource that's more valuable than money, and that's time. Since this book was free, let's look at it as a time investment.

Right now, you make a certain amount of money for every hour you work. Write down that number. Then, write down the number of hours it takes you to read this book. Multiply those numbers together, and that's how much of your time you invested in this book.

Let's say you get paid $10 an hour at your current job. If this book took you four hours to read, your equation should look like this.

$10/hour X 4 hours = $40

That's $40 worth of your precious time that you've invested so far, and I want you to earn that back.

By the end of this book, I want to increase what your time is worth. If I help you find consulting jobs where people pay you $100 an hour, now you've invested $400 of time in this book. As your time becomes more valuable, the way you spend it acquires more value as well. And I need to give you increasing value to keep up with you!

You don't have to be high-tech with your budgeting. There are some phenomenal apps, programs, software, and tools that will help you to track your ins and outs. Most of them cost money, so you may want to start with just a notebook.

My wife runs our hostel using a notebook to track the money coming in and going out. We have software that handles reservations, but she prefers to track money in a book. You can be as low-tech as you want, as long as you're tracking the right numbers.

The important thing is to see your time as valuable and your money as an investment rather than an expense. You didn't buy a business book; you invested in one. By spending $10 on a business book, you should expect to get back that $10 and even more.

This is how you're going to approach every dollar and every hour you invest in your new business from now on. By changing the way you talk about spending money, you will change your expectations.

PART II

BUSINESS MODELS

It's time to get to the meat of this book. I'm going to walk you through sixteen powerful and effective business models – many of which I use in my own business – that you can use to generate fast revenue, build runway, and develop passive income streams.

This is by no means an exhaustive list. These sixteen business models are designed to give you enough ideas to find one you connect with, but not so many that you feel overwhelmed.

I've seen other books that offer hundreds of ideas for business models. I prefer depth over breadth. I want to make sure you have a feel for each of these business models and see how you can use them to get started right away.

Take a look through these business models. Take your time trying to understand them and decide which ones could be the best fit for you.

BLOGGING

Blogging is how I first spread my wings on the Internet. I wrote my first blog post way back in 2007. More than a decade later, I still love blogging. It's like writing a diary entry that people like to read, comment on, and talk about.

Blogging is great because there are tons of people out there who would love to pay you to blog for them. I've seen services that provide three to five blog posts a month to start-ups and businesses. Some of those services charge thousands of dollars a month.

When you find your first client, you can charge them enough money to cover the cost of a killer blogging course. Once you learn the process and skills needed to be a great blogger, you can get more clients and charge more money.

When I think of the Internet, I think of Cookie Monster from Sesame Street. He has a voracious appetite and is constantly eating cookies. But, because he has no throat, every cookie he eats gets smashed in his mouth and bounces out, which means he only gets hungrier. He's like the Sisyphus of cookies, always pushing that cookie up the hill, only to have it fall right back down again.

The Internet is voracious in its desire for new content. Every day, readers are looking for what's new. We don't care about what happened last week or even yesterday; we want to know what's happening *now*.

This constant need for new content means there is a growing need for people to write blog posts.

While you're working for someone else and improving your blogging skills, you can begin to write posts for yourself. You start building out your own catalog, eventually, you can create your own blog. For less than $50, you can have a blog set up that will allow you to write posts for a year.

As your following grows, eventually, you no longer need to sell your time. Enough people are visiting your blog that you can now invest all your time in that passive revenue stream.

The best thing about blogging is that, when someone finds your blog and likes what they see, they're going to read your entire back catalog. When you start, you might feel like no one is reading your posts but just wait.

Soon, thousands of people are going to read everything you've ever written. This is how people engage in my content, and it's how I engage in content that I enjoy.

YOUTUBE

You don't have to be eloquent, fancy, or beautiful to be successful with videos. The biggest area for success on YouTube is actually videos for children. Children will watch the same videos for hours. My children love watching unboxing videos, which is basically just an advertisement for a toy. A little kid will open up toys and candy that they probably got for free, record the experience, and get paid to upload the video. My kids like watching those videos so much that, even when they own that toy, they would rather watch the video than play with the actual toy.

Most people make the mistake of thinking you have to be an expert in video marketing to succeed. In reality, the videos with the most views are the ones for beginners. Beginners need the most training, and they watch the most videos. A beginner video can get 100,000 views, whereas an advanced video might only get a few hundreds.

When I first started out way back in 2010, I thought I had to buy all the best tools. I bought a special video camera, a special microphone, a fancy tripod, expensive lighting, and even a background screen to set up behind me.

I have an entire multi-camera setup with all the bells and whistles, but I don't use any of it. I do almost all of my work using a four-year-old iPhone. The only equipment I have in addition to my iPhone is a Gimbal, which is a little holder that keeps the camera steady when I'm walking on the beach and a lavalier microphone that I plug into the phone and clip to my shirt.

It used to cost thousands of dollars to buy a studio, but now, you probably have all the equipment you need in your pocket without even realizing it.

Video marketing is a great chance to use your creativity, and this is an area of marketing that loads of businesses need help with. Most local businesses couldn't record a captivating video to save their lives.

A while back, there was a hotel in my hometown whose online presence was atrocious. They were paying a very expensive company to handle their online marketing; yet, if you clicked on the link to their website, it took you to a motel chain's website rather than their hotel's website.

I decided to send them a proposal, offering to help them improve their online presence. I wrote an extensive seventeen-page list of all the things that I would do to help that business grow.

Unfortunately, the woman who received my list was the one who had hired the marketing company that was ripping her off. Rather than admit that she had made a mistake, she sent back a very mean email, then proceeded to have the company she'd already hired implement my entire list.

She didn't want to admit what she had done wrong, so she continued to pay five or even ten times more than what I would have charged. The funniest part of the story is that the website is still terrible, even after they stole all of my ideas.

Their content is still boring, and they generate customers the exact same way hotels did in the 1980s. They don't do anything dynamic or creative.

I had an entire idea for a video marketing campaign that would have made them viral and would have doubled, tripled, or even quadrupled their business. I wrote a script about a hilarious murder mystery series that would take place in this hotel. It would be the type of advertising that no one else does, and it would have drawn attention.

This is what you can do. If you keep your videos fun and creative, you will smash all the other boring companies out of the market. Just like with blogging, you can create videos for clients and generate enough revenue while you're building your own channel.

INSTAGRAM

This book isn't going to cover every social media platform, but we are going to use Instagram as an example of how you can leverage social media to generate revenue.

Instagram is the most straightforward concept in the world. You take pictures, write a description, and other people can look at them. It's basically a way to show off.

When I first encountered Instagram, I thought I would take pictures of my kids, let my family follow me, and share the images without them being too public. Of course, that's not how anyone else uses the platform, and it shows just how much of a dad I've become.

The best way to use Instagram is to take pictures of yourself, use the filters to improve the photo and get people to follow you. If you get enough followers, a big brand might approach you and offer you $5,000 to $100,000 to take a picture of you holding their product.

Instagram is a business, not a game. It's a service you can provide for someone else while you build your own channel.

Most Instagram celebrities have someone else take their pictures using a camera that costs thousands of dollars. They then tweak the photo in Photoshop for hours until they look flawless. When they upload their picture, they strategically add tags to make sure it gets the maximum reach.

It's smoke and mirrors. That person did not get out of bed looking that beautiful, take a picture in the mirror before they hopped in the shower, and throw it online. They approach their Instagram account like a business, which they absolutely should. As I've said before, we want to approach everything as a business model.

They also cull constantly. Any photo that underperforms gets removed. If your average photo gets 2,000 likes, but one photo only has 500 likes, delete it; it's hurting your average.

This is why many of the most popular and successful channels only have 100 photos. It's not because they have only ever uploaded 100 photos; it's because they're continually pruning, tweaking, and improving their Instagram account. They see it as a business, and so should you.

As you start out, it's okay to take your own pictures with whatever camera you have. Along the way, you can learn the art of photography. You can master the lighting and angles until you become amazing at taking and editing photos. As you learn, you can begin building your own channel.

There are loads of businesses with underdeveloped Instagram channels. My own business has a very weak Instagram account. I only have so much time every day, and Instagram just seems to fall to the bottom of the list.

Over the past few years, I have hired three different women to run my Instagram channel, and each of them failed. I live on a tropical island. Right now, I'm standing in four inches of water. All I can see in front of me is two young boys paddling away in their canoe. Otherwise, it's paradise. Everywhere you look, the view is majestic. It would be nearly impossible for me to take a bad photo.

For my Instagram channel, I would take photos, send them to the girl, and ask her to upload them and add the hashtags. Each time, the person I hired put the images in the wrong size or the wrong shape, and there were countless spelling mistakes. It was amateur hour.

Even the people who are succeeding with other business models have opportunities where you can approach them and offer to help them in whatever area they're lacking. Along the way, you could build your own business in parallel.

I'm not saying this so that every person who reads this book emails me and offers to run my Instagram account. I'm merely pointing out that there are loads of people that you can approach who already have massive followings. Local businesses all need your help, and you can do something amazing for them.

11

AUTHOR

I write books for a living. Back when I wanted to build new businesses and generate revenue fast, I sold my time by ghostwriting for other people. Once I had enough revenue to sustain my business, I transitioned into passive income by writing books under my own name.

I first started using this model when I came to my paradise island. About five years ago, my wife and I came to this island on vacation for a month, and I immediately fell in love with it.

At the time, the power or the Internet would go out for two or five days at a time. I realized I couldn't have an active Internet business here. If I had a business where I had to be online every day, I'd be tearing my hair out every time the power cut out.

I wanted to switch to a heavily passive income stream, and that's when I transitioned to writing full-time.

I can write books when the power is out and when the Internet is turned off. I only need the Internet long enough to upload a book and send it to the client, the publisher, or whichever store is selling it.

The author model ties directly into so many other skills. Whether you're writing a blog post or a book, writing is writing. The better you get at writing, the more you can use it in other areas of your life.

When you're writing books for clients, you can try different methods and styles to get a feel for what people like and what they don't. Clients tend to give you fast feedback, so you'll know almost immediately if something didn't work.

When I work with a client on ghostwriting, I always explain my system. I create the overall structure, I get their approval, and then I add in the quotes, case studies, and personal stories. Of course, there are always some clients that don't listen. When I send them the rough draft, they always ask, "Why didn't you add this in?"

It can get frustrating working with clients who never listen to you, but it's very informative to listen to their complaints. When they're consistent, that tells you that every final book needs to have that element. They all want it, and there must be a reason why.

By writing books for other people in different markets, I become a better writer - I develop a better understanding of how to communicate with my audience, and I'm better able to train the writers who go through my programs so that they can accelerate faster.

Readers are always looking for more books. I read a book every day. Every month, I hop onto my Kindle, go to the science fiction section, and search for every single book on Kindle Unlimited released in the last thirty days. I read just about every single book with a review. As long one other person has read it, I'm willing to give it a shot.

I'm a consumer as well as a creator.

There are ways to accelerate the author business model

that can disconnect you from time faster. One of those ways is dictation.

Instead of typing out your book, you just speak it into a recorder, get it transcribed, clean it up, and send it off to your client.

A year and a half ago, I thought I was going blind. It was devastating. I switched to dictation so that I could continue to work and support my family even if I lost my vision.

Luckily, after going through a series of experiments and working through some processes of my own, I was able to reverse most of the problem. While the sword of Damocles still hangs over me, my eye problems seem to currently be in remission.

I'm constrained by how much time I can spend on a computer, but I can still dictate. That allows me to walk along the beach while I write my books, rather than sitting in a cave, typing away on a computer like I used to do.

The author business model is my favorite. It's where you can let your creativity fly, and it's where you have the most control of your destiny. There's an entire literary ecosystem where you can find a following and continue to put more books in front of them.

Rather than having to go out into the wilds of the Internet to hunt down fans, readers, and customers, you can build an entire business within that ecosystem.

12

PRODUCT CREATOR

A product creator is not quite the same thing as an author, but it's pretty similar. Products are what we sell in the direct response market, or directly from a website that seeks to solve a specific problem, and this is where I started before I switched into being an author.

As a product creator, you can help people, and you can generate revenue fast. Selling a book for $2.99 on Amazon is great, but it's not a lot of money. When you create a product, you can sell the same information for $47, and people will eat it up.

The only difference between a book and a product is the formatting. With a product, you can add images and make it look dynamic. When you become a master product creator, you create videos and audio to go along with your books.

The majority of the content I sell directly from my website is in the form of video training. I upload recordings of past training or new videos that I've recorded, and I add visuals to help my viewers follow along.

My process is very simple. I make slideshows using

Keynote on my Mac, and I add in cool images and transitions. I record videos where I talk about the same things I talk about in my books, I record that slideshow, and I end up with an awesome video.

Clients and customers are willing to pay four to five times more money for the exact same content in video format than they are in book format.

I used to have clients pay me to write books that they would sell in direct response. When I noticed that they would also pay someone else to take my book and turn it into a video, I realized that I was losing money by not knowing how to create videos. So, I took a few courses and taught myself to become a full-spectrum product creator.

These business models can all weave into each other. If you've already started working with video as part of your YouTube business model, combine that with the authorship business model, and you'll become a product creator.

There are plenty of marketers out there who are desperate for more products to sell to their audience. I'm constantly trying to create more products and more training to meet the needs of my following.

I'm a big believer in depth of catalog. Other people create one thing that works, and they ride that horse until it dies. They can make a lot of money, but it doesn't last forever. I'm much more of a believer of creating lots of useful things that work so that I constantly have an audience I can pivot toward.

As a product creator, you'll start off by getting paid a flat fee. Once you get better, you can start to ask for a percentage of profits. Then, you'll start having a passive revenue stream, getting paid even after your work is finished.

I wrote a book a few years ago that took me thirty-five hours of work. I asked for a percentage. Now, I get a direct deposit every single month for my royalties. I make far more money from the royalties than I would have made if they paid me a flat fee up front.

It took them a very long time to release that product, and I didn't make the first dollar for more than a year after I finished writing, but it still sells nearly every single day.

13

VOICEOVER ARTIST

Most of us know how to talk, and that's the only skill you need to get into this industry. The fastest growing segment of the book market is audiobooks.

Even though I dictate all of my books, the audio version of this book is not my voice. I don't have the patience or access to silence that I would need to record my own audiobooks.

I have plenty of clients who don't have an audio version of their books. They are leaving money on the table and ignoring the need of people who prefer that format. When I ask them why they don't meet that need, they always say that they want to record it themselves, but they're just waiting for the right time.

Let me tell you a secret: if you're waiting for the right time, it's never going to come.

Despite the fact that I have a podcast and dictate all of my books, creating an audiobook is outside of my skill set. In the background of all my recordings, there's the rustling of palm trees, the roar of the motorcycles, and the splashing of waves.

All of those background noises would drive people crazy when listening to an audiobook. In fact, the audiobook checkers would never let it through.

Fortunately, a dictation recording doesn't have to sound perfect, and my following is kind enough to enjoy the tropical background noises in my podcast episodes.

You can make a lot of money in the voice-over industry, and you don't need a lot of equipment. You can use your first paycheck to buy a better microphone and some sound-proofing for your home studio. As you get more jobs, you can raise your prices to fund better equipment.

My friend Adam is a very successful voice-over artist who mostly focuses on business recordings. He charges more than sixty times what beginning voice-over artists get paid, and that's the bottom of his fee structure.

There's no ceiling on this industry because the need for audio content is growing. It's outpacing the demand for other types of content, and I believe there will be even more opportunities in this market moving forward.

We live busy lives. Whether you're driving to work, riding the subway, or traveling on a plane, many of us want to listen to content instead of reading it. Sometimes, we want to give our eyes a break.

As you continue to work for clients, you'll improve your skills and be able to buy better equipment. You can, then, harness your newly-honed abilities and do the voice-overs for your own book, start your own podcast, or create your own course to teach other people how to be voice-over artists.

Every single one of my books has an audio version. Instead of paying a flat fee, I prefer to share the royalties of all my audiobooks with the people who created them. This is an excellent opportunity for them to build passive revenue streams.

The English guy who did the voice recording for *Serve No Master* is feeling pretty good about that. While I'm continually working, buying traffic, and getting more people to learn about my brand, his work is finished. He did his job, and it's a win for both of us.

14

PODCASTER

I don't consume very many audiobooks. Many of my followers love them, but whenever I try to listen to a book, I fall asleep. It doesn't matter how many spies or robots are running around.

Podcasts, on the other hand, are my favorite way to engage entertainment. I could listen to podcasts all day long. When I find a new show I like, I listen to the entire back catalog, whether it's dozens or even hundreds of episodes.

There are so many ways to enter the world of podcasting as a business, the most obvious being the presenter and voice of the show. However, there are plenty of behind-the-scenes roles you can take on.

You could be a producer or an editor; you could book guests for the show, including celebrities or experts; you could write the script; you could record the intro, outro, and commercials; you could control the audio levels; you could control the technology and upload the finished product. There are so many elements that go into creating a good podcast.

Once you find your role in a podcast, there's a simple

format to go from zero to a big show – interview the biggest guests.

One of my good friends gets 2.5 million downloads every single month for his podcast. When he first started, he was interviewing his friends who had followings in the hundreds. Now, he only interviews people who have followings in the millions. He has been on my show, but there's no way I could ever be on his again.

If you have one hundred fans, it's enough to start getting guests on your podcast. Message the people you're interested in working with and tell them why you want to interview them and how it will benefit them.

Whenever I want someone to cooperate with me on a project, I say, "I want to share your message to my audience." That's something everyone wants to hear.

When you're first starting out, interview someone with a following of around one hundred people. When they appear on your show, they'll tell their fans about it, and those excited fans will start to be a part of your audience.

While you're working on other people's shows to generate revenue, you can build your own show at the exact same time. When you buy new equipment or learn a new skill, those tools and training can be used on your own projects.

Podcasting is the easiest way to generate content, and it's my favorite part of my business. I don't get to record podcasts nearly as much as I'd like to because I spend so much time creating other content for my following, but I've already outlined fifty-two episodes that I want to record next year.

You can get into this business model without having to buy new things. I have a very expensive podcasting setup with a fancy microphone, a thick XLR cable, and an impressive audio recorder. I don't use any of it.

The same microphone and phone that I use to record my videos and dictate my books are what I use to record my podcast, and you can do the same. All you need is a recording device and your voice.

The more you practice recording your voice, the better you'll get at it. My recordings now are far better than they were five years ago. Getting better at podcasting helped me to get better at dictating, and it can help you get better as a voice-over artist.

Podcasting perfectly dovetails with many of the other projects I've already talked about. If you're recording videos on YouTube or working as a voice-over artist, you're already using your voice.

While each of these business models is enough to stand on their own, they can easily tie into any of the other business models.

You can choose two or three that all help to strengthen each other. That way, even if one of those business models falls away, you can still lean heavily into another model and continue to generate a passive revenue stream.

15

COPYWRITING

C opywriting is, hands down, the fastest way to get rich online, and it is the most valuable skill that you can develop in isolation to ensure your financial future.

Copywriting is simply the ability to write something that motivates the reader or the listener to take action. A great example of this is writing an ad that appears in a magazine. When someone sees that ad, they buy that car or watch.

Copywriting is a universal skill. If the Internet ever collapses, copywriting will continue to exist.

To master the art of copywriting, a great exercise is to look at old ads. I have a ton of ads from the early 1900s and the late 1800s that I can share with you through my website. There are some fantastic ads from around 1901 that are so powerful, you can copy them almost word for word, and they'll still work today.

I don't like to copy modern ads for a couple of reasons. First, they're still in copyright. If you take something from someone else's sales letter or commercial, it is stealing. Anything written after about 1940 is in the danger zone.

The copyright law is constantly getting pushed back for one reason, and that reason is Mickey Mouse. Disney is making sure that that little mouse never falls out of copyright. If he did, anyone could make a Mickey Mouse movie, just like anyone today can make a Sherlock Holmes movie.

I like older ads also because of how hard it used to be to get a product. To buy this book, you went to a website, you clicked a button, and you entered your email address. The book was delivered directly to your e-device or by email.

It used to be much more complicated.

Back in 1910, you would write a book on how to make someone sound smarter to impress the people around them. Then, you would have to put ads in a magazine or newspaper with headlines like, "Tired of sounding like a dummy? Want to sound smarter? Want people to think you're educated? Want to impress future employers?"

If your ad was well-designed, people would begin the process of buying your book. They would cut out your ad, check a box on it, and fill out all the information with their home address. They would then go to the bank to get a cashier's check.

For those of you who don't know what a cashier's check is, let me explain. You would give the bank a certain amount of money, and the cashier would create a piece of paper that was worth that specific amount of money. That piece of paper could only be cashed by the person you sent it to. The check was guaranteed by the bank, not you.

After they received the check, they would go to the post office, buy an envelope, put the stamps on it, and put everything inside that envelope. If the book needed a self-addressed, stamped envelope, they would even have to buy two envelopes and two sets of stamps. They would mail everything to you, and six to eight weeks later, their new book on how to talk smarter would arrive.

Nobody on earth would go through that process now. To buy a book today only takes seconds to go through a process that used to take an entire day.

When I look at these older ads, I know they're powerful because they got people to do a lot more. This book is free and takes only a few seconds to be delivered directly to you, and I still have to fight to get people to download and read it. Yet copywriters a century ago were able to get people to leave their homes and do all that work just to buy a book from them.

The beauty of copywriting is that you get paid in accordance with your ability. There are loads of small jobs that pay $100 or $200 that you can take when you're just getting started. Once you hone your skills and master the art of copywriting, you can take jobs that pay tens of thousands of dollars.

To become a great copywriter, you should take a small course. I offer a free beginner's course on my website that can give you tons of amazing resources.

There are over 600 old ads in my Ultimate Swipe File. Copy each of them down by hand into a notebook, making sure to read and engage in each of them. This will allow you to grasp the idea of a good ad.

Once you get a feel for the structure, you can start taking low-ticket jobs. As with the other business models, you can use the money you earn to pay for more advanced courses so that you can get paid even more.

When you reach a certain level, you can become an apprentice. I've been an apprentice, and I've even had my own apprentices.

One of the best things about being an apprentice is that

all the clients that are outside your mentor's budget get sent to you. When you run into hiccups, you ask your mentor for help, they tweak your work, and you learn along the way.

Copywriting is ninety percent structure and ten percent fancy words. Most people focus on the fancy words first, and they never get anywhere.

Fancy words aren't as crucial in copywriting because we don't respond to polished messages as much as we used to. When a message feels too polished or too fancy, it starts to feel artificial.

I tend to write in a way that my followers respond to. I tell real stories using the way I talk to my friends and family. I like to say what I'm feeling and talk about what's really happening in my life.

When I'm recording a video, I grab my phone and my gimbal, I walk along the beach, and my basic structure is, "Here's what this product is. Here's what it does. Here's how it can help you. Here's why I think it's worth it. Here's why you should take action right now." It's a simple structure, it resonates well with the listeners, and it's still an excellent copywriting technique.

As a copywriter, the possibilities are endless. You can write local ads for the newspaper, for the yellow pages, or for Craigslist, and you can go into the realm of writing radio or local TV commercials, which is very fun.

This is a universal skill that works in every single market and medium of communication, and it's an amazing way to quickly generate revenue.

As you move to the higher echelons of copywriting, you start to get into passive revenue streams by getting paid a percentage of the success.

Some of the biggest copywriters in the world will go to multi-million-dollar businesses and ask for 50 percent of the improvement. If a previous ad was generating $1 million, while your ad generates $2 million, you could split that additional $1 million 50/50.

You might be thinking, "Oh my gosh, they're paying someone half a million dollars." That business is actually thinking, "We're going to make an extra half a million dollars."

I absolutely love the craft of copywriting. It's future-proof, it's technology-proof, and it's an easy skill to learn.

16

AFFILIATE MARKETER

Affiliate marketing is an intriguing business. In simplest terms, as an affiliate, you get paid for recommending things.

For example, if you visit my website and click the link to my book *Serve No Master* on Amazon, Amazon will pay me a percentage of that sale as the affiliate. It's not a lot of money, but it's some extra money on top of the royalties I receive for being the product creator.

If you go to servenomaster.com/toolbox, I list the tools that I use for my business. If you want to know about the microphone I use or the host for my website, I have links, pictures, and explanations for everything I use.

Almost all of those links are affiliate links. If you like a tool I'm using and click on the link I provide to buy that product, I get paid a percentage of that sale.

Traffic is very precious, and being an affiliate is mostly just generating traffic for a product. You're sending a business a new customer, and that's incredibly valuable.

I have extensive training on how to be an affiliate marketer, and I teach people the skills they need to recommend products they believe in. Of course, I provide a lot of training on how to recommend my products specifically because I want as big an audience as I can possibly get.

Here's how much I'll pay you to send anyone my way. I'll give you half of everything they spend with me for eternity. If they spend $7 this week, I'll send you $3.50. If in ten years they spend $10,000, I'll send you $5,000.

That's how valuable affiliate marketing is to me, and I'm by no means the only business who will do this.

Loads of online businesses pay for recommendations all the time. Have you ever wondered why it seems like every podcast has similar commercials? They don't all believe in that mattress or that website builder. They're simply affiliates.

When you see or hear, "Use this special link or promo code," that's how you know someone is an affiliate. These links and codes are how businesses follow where traffic came from, and it's how they know which customers are yours.

This is a business model used in real life. When you walk past a comedy club or a nightclub, you've probably seen someone standing on the street, holding a flyer and telling you to come to this club.

If you look closely, there's a marking on the flyer to let them know which person sent you. When you go to that club and pay to get in, they know how many people were generated by each representative based on the flyers.

As an online affiliate marketer, you can start out by recommending the products that you already use. Tell your friends about a movie you love, share a link, and earn some money when they buy the film.

You can even partner with other people and have an affiliate team.

There are a lot of products I use that I don't have enough time to write reviews for. When I write a review of a product, I like to use a lot of screenshots and walkthroughs to go in depth.

Because I can't use the computer very much, I'm always looking for people to partner with me on writing reviews for products that I believe in. When I earn money from those reviews, the people who wrote it also get paid.

Just like the other business models, when you start writing reviews for the products you use, you can decide to get paid a flat fee or a percentage of what your review generates.

With affiliate marketing, you can start immediately. You don't need traffic, and you don't need a product. You can jump right in and start writing your review.

I have an entire walkthrough and blog post on my website about how to write a fantastic review that will generate traffic all by itself.

You can start by reviewing products that not a lot of other people talk about. Your review will go right to the top of the page because you're the only one there. Even if you're not great at reviewing, you'll still be at the top of the charts, and you'll be the top affiliate for that product.

Businesses are always looking for more affiliates. It's a growing market, and it's only going to get bigger.

More social media platforms are getting into this market, as well. When you become popular on Instagram and build up a following of 10,000 people or more, you can start doing some cool things.

When you take a selfie wearing your cutest outfit, Instagram will let you mark each thing you're wearing. Someone could click on your shirt, and it will take them to a website where they can buy it.

Using this technology, you're no longer just recommending a shirt; you get paid for every person who saw your picture and bought what you're wearing.

This industry ties into every single other business model we've already talked about. You can recommend products on your blog, on your YouTube channel, or on your podcast. From a simple review, you can start earning money from the products you use.

17

NETWORKER

The majority of my revenue comes from networking. My technical skills are decent, but everything I teach, everything I do, and everything I am is a commodity.

There's nothing about me that's unique. There are people that look like me, and there are people with the same name as me. I'm not even sure if I'm in the top ten of the most famous Jonathan Greens.

I have the skills I need to succeed, but it's not my technical prowess that has moved me to success in my industry. My success comes from my ability to meet, connect, and forge business deals within an hour of meeting everyone I encounter.

I teach almost everything I know about networking for free on my blog and in my podcast episodes. I've written plenty of books on this topic, and I have advanced courses to help you become a better networker.

You don't need technical skills to succeed in networking; all you need is the ability to meet people and forge a connection. If you're an extrovert, this is your dream job. For the rest of us introverts, I have some tips on how to use socializing to improve your business.

I travel to two to three conferences a year to grow my business. Now that I have a family, I don't travel very often away from my island. In every direction I look, there are palm trees. Even if I didn't have a family, why would I ever want to leave Paradise Island?

When I do leave, I require maximum efficiency to take advantage of every minute I'm away from home.

Here's my simple process for networking. I go out, and I meet people. For every person I meet, I find out who they are, what they love, and what they need to grow their business. I save that information in my head. You could even write it down in a journal or an app on your phone.

As I build up my contact list, I start to look for connections between the people I know. Whenever I meet two people that would match well together, I connect them with each other. If person A is looking for a copywriter and person B is a copywriter looking for work, I introduce them so that they can do business together.

The more people you help, the more people that will want to help you back.

In my industry, the online marketing world, the standard commission for an introduction is ten to twenty percent. If you introduce two people with a huge following and an amazing product and they end up generating $1 million in sales, you will get paid $100,000 just for that introduction.

I have a friend, David, whose entire job is to introduce people. He goes to conferences and throws parties, meeting as many people as possible to continue to grow his contact list. When he meets someone that would be a good match for an existing contact of his, he makes the introduction and waits for the revenue to come back his way.

Other than keeping in touch with people, he doesn't do anything. He doesn't have a website, he doesn't have a blog, and he's not recording podcast episodes. He's simply in the middle, and it's incredible.

I'm always looking for more introductions. When someone sends me a person I could work with, I'm more than happy to pay that commission.

This is how I generate all of my other work. All of my ghostwriting clients come to me through these connections. When a friend messages me asking if I'm available for a copywriting job, a ghostwriting job, or a book launch, they send me a client, and I pay that person for connecting us.

If you visit my website, you'll notice there's no landing page for ghostwriting or any of my other services. My schedule is so full that I don't have to reach out to clients; clients have to reach out to me.

I spent a long time putting together examples of my previous work to demonstrate the successes I have and all the past projects I've done.

Most people who hire me do not look at my resume. They say, "So-and-so said you're good. We're just going to hire you." The truth is, I hire people that way, too. If someone comes with a recommendation from someone I trust, I tend to give them the job.

Not only can networking function as introductions between people, but it's also a chance to hone in on your other business model skills. Networking will help you find affiliates, jobs, and partners to help you manage the different aspects of your business.

18

FASHION MOGUL

This model is basically printing on demand. You use a website builder as your software and a print-on-demand company as your delivery. There are a lot of businesses that do exactly this.

I'm a big believer in the on-demand economy. I like to sell things that don't exist until after I get paid. When you buy the paperback edition one of my books, it doesn't go to the printing press until your credit card payment clears.

Using this model, you make less money per sale, but you also have no risk. You don't have a thousand copies of a book sitting in a warehouse somewhere. Instead, you have the information available in whatever format your customer prefers, whether it be an audiobook, paperback, or e-book.

In this business model, you can leverage a single skill. In fact, you don't even need that.

I originally started designing t-shirts and hats with "Serve No Master" written on them because I wanted to wear them.

I wear a lot of baseball hats. Every once in a while, a box of old baseball hats ends up for sale at the local market, and

I grab any of the hats that fit my head. I realized that, if I'm going to be advertising something on the top of my head, it might as well be my own brand.

That's when I started getting curious about printing my own hats and shirts. I have a website where I have t-shirts that I've designed available for sale. I'm not any good at design. I can tell you what I want, but I need an artist to take it across the finish line.

Every single t-shirt on my website was designed by someone else. I came up with the idea, showed the designer a stock photo of what I want it to look like, and let them create the drawing.

By using Shopify and a print-on-demand company, I don't have to do anything else. Visitors go to the website, they buy whatever they like, and it gets delivered to them. Everything's handled by someone else, and a little money ends up in my bank account.

This is a great business to get into, and plenty of people are leaning into it. Best of all, it's a growing market that you can jump right into. All you have to do is create a drawing or hire someone to draw your idea.

You can now sell your shirts directly through Amazon, and they'll print them for you, too. I have a few shirts that I sell this way. At any given time, I have between three and five designs for sale directly on Amazon, designed by me and printed by them. I upload the design, and they do the rest.

If you don't know how to start, you can start by working for someone else. You can create designs for someone else that they sell through their website, or you can work on managing another person's website.

I haven't taken my clothing line nearly as far as I want to. I have plenty of designs and ideas, but not enough time to implement them. I would love to have someone help me set up my clothing line.

If you're artistic or interested in e-commerce, this is a business route you can enter. It's growing massively, and there are tons of opportunities.

There are a lot of micro-sites out there that only sell one type of shirt, whether it be political, hunting, or sports t-shirts. People prefer to engage with a smaller website where every single product matches what they're into, and this is where there's opportunity for you.

19

DROPSHIPPING

Dropshipping is very similar to the print-on-demand t-shirt business, except you don't have to do any designing. This is where you find a product someone else made, and you sell it from your website for a little bit more.

The difference between dropshipping and print-on-demand is that, with dropshipping, the product already exists when you order it. There's already a warehouse that someone else is paying for filled with this product that you're now selling.

This means that it gets delivered a little bit faster, but there's also not as much customization for the customer.

People do this all the time where I live. I can find a product on my country's version of Amazon; then, I can find the same product on a Chinese manufacturing website for a little bit less.

All the dropshipper does is take my order, order the same product from China, and have them ship it directly to me. A lot of packages arrive with the Chinese labels still on them.

This is something you can do. Find something designed by other people and sell it. This is very similar to being an affiliate, except you get a much higher percentage by generating the traffic for someone else's product.

As a dropshipper, you control a more substantial part of the supply or sales chain. Rather than handing off the customer to the website, you go through the entire transactional process. Someone visits your website, they place the order, they send you the money, and you use that money to place the dropshipping order.

You are part of the engagement window, which means you get paid proportionately more when you work as a dropshipper than you would as an affiliate, especially for physical products. Affiliates for physical products make low commissions where dropshippers to make a lot.

There are a lot of things that you can buy for $1 in China and sell for a $100 in America. That's a pretty good profit margin.

The market seems to be shifting toward dropshipping. A lot of the products you see for sale on Amazon are dropshipped. Do you ever wonder why there are fifty plastic spoons that all look very similar to each other? They're all made in the same factory, but sold by different people, a.k.a. the dropshippers.

In fact, most laptops, paddle boards, and other products are all made in the same factory. No matter which brand you're buying, they're all made at the same place. It makes sense because they're the experts on it.

Networking comes in handy when you're trying to get involved in the dropshipping business.

You could find someone who's already in the business, and find a place where you can slot yourself into their business, whether it's copywriting, generating customers, writing blog posts or even creating a podcast all about amazing mugs that this company has to sell.

If you live in Asia, as I do, you could start to leverage connections. If you have contacts in China or you know how to speak Chinese or Hindi, you could go to the countries where these main factories are, and you can dig deep to become very successful in this market.

Your ability to meet and connect with people in other countries will open up more opportunities and more doors.

20

LOCAL DIGITAL SERVICES

The first money I ever made online was for SEO (search engine optimization) for a local massage therapist in my hometown. For the first three months, she paid me $200 a month, then $500 a month for the rest of our professional relationship.

All I did was use my Internet skills to attract attention to her business and boost the quantity of traffic to her website. We recorded videos, posted them onto YouTube, and got people in our area looking at them. I helped get her Google Places listing at the top of the charts, and I helped her website appear at the top of their search results.

Remember when I said you should always try to get paid three times for each job? I took that first paycheck and bought a course on how to do SEO. I took the second paycheck and bought software. I used that course and software to get more clients who were paying me more money.

By the time I was finished, I was charging $2,000 a month for the same service. As an expert at SEO, I could charge a higher fee rather than the fake-it-till-you-make-it price.

There are loads of businesses in your area that have a terrible online presence.

One of my friends from high school runs a successful chain of gymnasiums. I was a member there until I moved away.

The first time I drove past one of his gyms, I remembered that he was the owner. I pulled out my iPhone and looked up his website, only to discover that the technology he used to build the website wasn't iPhone compatible.

This was a large business with a growing number of franchises, yet, half the smartphone users in the world couldn't visit his website.

The same thing happened with a guitar store near my hometown. It had one of the most beautiful websites I'd ever seen, but it was designed with such old technology that most browsers today won't even load.

He paid a lot of money for that website. He didn't realize that, even though it looked beautiful, it was designed in a way that's no longer compatible with today's technology.

There are tons of local businesses who don't know how to turn a visitor into a customer, and some of them don't even appear on the search results.

When I was hired by the massage therapist, her biggest problem was that no one ever called her from the website. When I checked it out, I immediately saw why no one called. Her phone number wasn't even on the website.

Her web designer had made a massive mistake, and I see this all the time.

I can't even tell you how many times I wanted to buy something but couldn't find the contact details on the website. I search in the footnotes of the website to find the details and end up being linked to a fake email address that's never been customized.

I've seen plenty of big-name authors in my industry who have the same problem. They have been on television shows and have a massive following, yet their contact form is broken.

It doesn't matter how big the business is. There are a lot of opportunities for you to reach out to someone and offer them your help. If you see an area where you can help accelerate their business or improve their online presence, you can always reach out to them and offer your services.

Once you improve your skills and know what a good online presence should look like, you can move into the realm of arbitrage – buying internationally, selling locally.

As I grew my business and raised my prices, eventually, I stopped doing the technical work myself. I was just a salesperson and a client manager, and I would find someone else in another country to do the grunt work.

I'd find a client, they would pay me a fee, and I would pay a percentage of that fee to someone else to do all the work. There are massive profit margins in the eighty to ninety percent range when you go this route.

Again, we're building on the techniques of local networking. Getting local clients is not hard. I started out just posting ads on Craigslist. You can post ads on LinkedIn or go to local meetups and events for small business owners.

By using your networking skills, you could find a lot of businesses that are struggling. If they don't improve their websites, figure out social media, and figure out how to reach audiences using today's technology, they're going to start disappearing.

When I was growing up, video stores were locally owned. Often, a local convenience store would have a video section in the back of the store.

Eventually, one large company came in with lower prices

and caused all of these locally-owned stores to shut down. Of course, once they shut down all the competition, they raised the prices back up and made a massive amount of money.

Then, the market shifted once again. A new company came around, offering to mail DVDs right to your house. You didn't even have to leave your home to watch the movies you wanted. The big business that shut down all of the local video stores got shut down by the next person who figured out how the Internet worked.

Adapting to the Internet is critical for businesses to grow. By offering your services and knowledge of the Internet, you aren't just making money; you're saving local businesses. You're giving them a chance to compete with big corporations.

Just as before, this model is a way to hone the skills you've already learned. You can learn how to write copy and how to run a social media account to improve the presence of local businesses that desperately need your services. Along the way, you're learning and improving skills that, simultaneously, can be used in your own business.

21

GRAPHICS

I f you're not good with computers and technology, maybe you're good with graphics. I certainly wish I was. There are plenty of opportunities for artists, and you don't have to know a thing about programming.

I work with an artist who designs beautiful sales pages, but he doesn't know anything about computer programming. He creates a drawing, which he sends to me, then a programmer takes that drawing and turns it into a webpage.

There are so many possibilities if you know how to draw. A beautiful thing to do with graphics is simply drawing designs for coloring books.

Coloring books, especially adult coloring books, are an exploding market. I'm always putting out new coloring books for precisely this reason. I was teaching my wife about the market, but she became busy running our hostel. I guarantee you that, the second my daughter's hands are steady enough, she's going to continue running our coloring book business.

If you're someone with a natural artistic ability, you can draw by hand and scan it into a computer, or you can draw directly into the computer. Whatever way you choose, you can design websites, t-shirts, or even logos to sell to other people.

Every single thing on my website was designed by someone else. I paid someone a lot of money to create a logo for me, and he did an amazing job. I paid someone else to look at a picture of me and make me into a drawing in the same style as the rest of my website; she also did an amazing job.

I hire graphic designers all the time. In fact, I have a full-time graphic service I work with. I have hundreds of small graphics tasks that I always need to have taken care of, so having a service on hand is a great way to save time searching for artists.

There are so many new businesses that need everything from business cards, logos, and book covers to t-shirts, drawings, and comic books. If you have artistic ability, you can lean heavily into this.

Start by doing graphics and design work for other people. You can use this work to get a feel for what works and what doesn't. Not everything that's beautiful works well online, and working with clients is a great way to experiment.

Once you master your craft and know how to create a killer design online, you can move onto your own business to design a great-looking website and sales page.

One of the coolest things you can do is create assets for other people to use. I once worked with a graphic designer to create an entire catalog of assets. This simply means the arrows, logos, stamps, colors, and backgrounds that people use on their websites.

We created this massive collection of different graphics, and we sold hundreds of units in a single weekend.

This is what you could do as a graphic artist. Once you create a whole collection of useful assets, you can start to sell them. You could have a web designer start-up kit or templates that go with specific website designs. These assets only need to be created once, but they can be sold repeatedly.

There is a considerable market for PowerPoint and Keynote templates. I buy templates all the time. Every time I create a new course or a new product, I buy a new template. I want to make sure that each course looks distinct from my other products.

When you create these assets, you can sell them through large websites that handle everything for you. You can also put your drawings on stock photo websites. You can sell the same content on a lot of different platforms to generate long-term, passive income.

You can use the money from your initial clients to hone your skills and buy you the runway you need to start building the things you want to sell long-term.

You don't have to be in the services industry to be in the graphics industry; you can sell graphics as a product. I buy a lot of stock images, photographs, and graphics, but I also hire a lot of graphic artists to customize those.

There are so many opportunities there, not just in selling your designs. You could teach your skills. There are loads of tutorials teaching people how to use graphics software or how to draw in a particular style. Whether you sell your designs or sell your knowledge, you will be able to pour more revenue into your central business.

22

SOFTWARE DEVELOPER

We've now moved into the advanced business models that only a small percent of the people who read this book can dive into.

Software development is a growing part of the market. There are loads of schools that will teach you how to code and learn the process to become a front-end or back-end developer. These are all skills that you can learn.

The reason everyone wants to learn to be a developer is that there are so many companies that are desperate to hire you and pay you the big bucks. All those large social media companies that are buying and selling each other need more people to code and build their products.

Working for a big company is one way to go, but you can start off a lot simpler.

I have an app that helps you design a book description for Amazon. It's custom-designed to only use the HTML that Amazon allows.

There is a full template, and all you have to do is fill in the areas, click some buttons, and make your book description look amazing. Once you fill out the information, you enter your email address, and it sends you an eternal copy of the code that you can copy and paste into Amazon.

I didn't know how to build that app. I came up with the idea, and someone else built it for me over a couple of days.

Little apps like that are super valuable. You don't always need to go for the big projects; there are plenty of programs and opportunities where you can insert yourself to truly help people.

I've always struggled with adding subtitles to my videos. Recently, however, I found a free tool that just inserts the subtitles for me.

I love this tool so much, in fact, that I emailed the founder with some changes he could make to drastically improve his tool. When he replied to me, I found out that he's just starting out. I told him that, if he made the changes I suggested, he could start to sell his tool for a lot of money.

Whether you come from the IT world or you've been building apps and software for big companies, you don't have to develop massive programs to generate revenue online. There are a lot of small tools that are really useful.

I don't know why, but it's incredibly difficult to convert video and audio formats. I recently found a new tool that simply converts your video into any format you want.

Before, when I wanted to make a PDF file, it would be too big. I would have to upload it to a website, re-download it in the right size, then re-upload it to a different website to clean off all the tracking data.

Now that I've found this tool, I can convert files with the click of a button. It's tools like this where the opportunity lies for developers.

Many authors struggle with formatting their books. For so long, I had to manually format my books, and it was a nightmare. I was so frustrated that I started talking to developers about building my own piece of software to solve my problem. Finally, someone came up with a really good piece of software that I use to format my books on Mac, but they don't have a PC version.

What I struggle with now is formatting coloring books. The process I go through for formatting a coloring book starts off with creating a PowerPoint presentation in the wrong size. Then, I have to take all of the text pages, convert those to PDF, drag and drop those onto the PowerPoint presentation, and then drag and drop the images for each coloring book page.

I have to make minor adjustments, and then I upload them to Amazon. Every single time, some of the images aren't right, and I have to go back and tweak them. It's a total nightmare. I would love to have a program that makes it easy to format coloring books.

There are places where people have a need, and, as a developer, you can go in and develop small pieces of software to make life easier for everyone else.

You can start off by finding people like me, who have specific problems that we need solved. You could get a list of my ideas and partner with me to build something that we can sell.

Once you've worked with enough people, you can start making your own side projects that will, eventually, turn into your own software that you can sell. Even better, you could rent your service for a monthly fee. That's when you start to have a very successful business with a lot of money rolling in.

23

WEB DESIGNER

The person who designs the graphics for a website is not the same person who puts everything together. A graphic designer knows how to make amazing drawings, but the web designer knows about front-end development, which is the website that customers see.

The only reason why web designer is last on this list is that it's a specialized, technical skill. Either you know how to do it, or you don't. You can certainly become self-taught, but it will take you some time to learn what you need to know.

There are a lot of opportunities for a custom web designer. This is a growing market in which you can make a tremendous amount of money.

Remember the massage therapist who paid me $200 a month? She had paid $5,000 to the web designer who built her a website that didn't have her phone number on it.

When I logged into the back end, I discovered it was a template that the web designer had bought for $49. He spent one day customizing and tweaking the colors on that template, then collected a 99 percent profit margin.

As a web designer, you could start off doing custom websites for local businesses. You can customize templates built by other people, or you can design templates to go with different web designing themes.

You can even build child themes. These are websites that only work if someone buys the other website theme. There are a lot of businesses making seven, eight, and nine figures that sell this type of technology. This is a massive part of the market.

Plenty of large companies will pay you $100,000 to design their website. This is clearly a growing market.

Think about all the websites out there that are getting redesigned year after year or all the new businesses that are putting up their first website. These people know what content they want, but they don't have the technical skills to make it happen. They would be happy to pay you to put their vision into reality.

I redesign my website about once a year. I'm always adding changes, cleaning up the design, creating a new feel, or trying to get a faster interface.

The person who designed my website about two versions ago is now far outside what I can afford on a website redesign. The last time I talked to him, his prices had quadrupled, and I'm sure that, by now, his rates are even higher.

Just as he improved his skills, so, too, can you. Just think – after a few years of designing small websites, you could start to charge hundreds of thousands of dollars. As you begin to build up your list of clients and your history, you can raise your prices and build yourself a really nice website.

In order to go passive with the skill, you should start to

sell your expertise as a service to build runway. Then, you can start to develop assets, tools, and templates and record tutorials and training videos for other people. This will get you into the passive revenue streams.

24

ONCE YOU'VE CHOSEN YOUR PATH

I 've now shared with you sixteen amazing online business models, and I hope that one of them appeals to you. What we're going to do now is make a plan.

The reason most new businesses fail is that there is no plan. There's no goal, so it's impossible to count and track their progress. We're not going to let that happen with your business.

The first step of your plan is to determine how much runway you need to build. Runway is measured by two metrics – time and money.

How much time do you have to invest in this project? How many hours per day or per week can you spend working on building your business? How much money do you need to make before this can become your full-time venture?

I like to use three financial measures:

1. Your side venture is generating enough revenue that it removes the financial stress from your life.

That means that, if every month your debt is increasing by $100, you need to make $100 a month from this new business venture. That will take you from increasing your debt to breaking even. It might not sound exciting to break even, but it's much better than adding to your debt.

2. You're generating enough revenue to quit your primary job. Right now, you make a certain amount of money per month working for someone else. Imagine if you were able to make that amount by working on your new side business.

Once you start making the same amount of money working two hours at your new business as you do by working eight hours at your main job, you've quadrupled what an hour of your time is worth.

If you were making $100 a day working eight hours, now you can make $100 a day working two. When you quit that other job and start working full-time at your new job, you can accelerate that to $400 a day.

3. You increase what you make per hour. When I think about a raise, I don't think of the traditional raise of a dollar an hour or 2 percent per year.

To me, a raise is a number followed by the letter X. A raise is when you double, triple, or quadruple your income. That's how you need to start thinking.

As you begin building your business model, you have to start by knowing your numbers. How much money do you need to quit your job? In other words: how much money do you need until you have real runway?

Once you're generating money from a service in which you sell your time using one of these business models, you can quit your day job and use those eight hours every day to build passive income streams.

You might spend a few hours every day building websites for someone else. However, the rest of your day should be spent building assets for your website that you can sell directly. This is the business model that we're building here.

Pick one of these sixteen business models and dive into it. Grab it with both hands, and start looking at real numbers. Once you know how much money you need to make to build your runway, you need to check how much time and money it will cost you to master this craft.

If you don't know anything about computers, and you want to learn web designing or programming, you have a lot of training to go through. If you start with a skill that you already have, like my friend, Adam, who has a great voice, you can dive right into podcasting or audiobooks.

The danger that I want you to avoid is falling in love with all sixteen business models. It's very tempting to fall into Shiny Object Syndrome, where you get excited about all the different possibilities.

Don't try to learn more than one at a time. Stick with one model until it makes money. When you have a business model that is financially viable, you can start to learn a second one.

For each of these business models, I have extensive free training on my website. There are podcast episodes, blog posts and training videos that are available to you for free. Please, use these tools to master and understand your new craft.

Writing and selling books is the core of my business model. I've been through every course out there, and I'm constantly signing up for new courses whenever I find one. I'm continually trying to be an expert in my field.

Expertise is the game changer. You should be so dedicated to your new business that you are constantly trying to find new information.

So far, you haven't spent any money yet. Your only

investment is the value of your time, and I want you to earn that investment back.

Dive into your business model. Be proactive and make a commitment to your new business. Promise yourself that you're going to stick with it until you hit your first financial goal. When you reach that first goal, you're going to experience a level of excitement that you never thought was possible. That excitement will drive you to continually strive to be better at your craft.

I hope you're starting to feel a little bit of that excitement and hope now. You have to realize that you can do this. Your life is going to get better, but you have to take that first step and make the commitment.

Unlike a lot of other books, I'm not going to promise you that your life can change without any work. Sometimes, people get lucky and fall into something, but I don't believe in luck.

Instead of banking on lady luck, I want you to focus on consistent work to generate consistent reward.

25

HEROES VERSUS FAILURES

There are plenty of people who are looking for any excuse to quit. Some people will download this book, but never open it; there are others who will start reading this book, but never finish it; there are even some people who will finish this book, but never take action.

I don't want you to be one of those people.

At the end of one of my programs or courses, there is always someone who messages me to complain that the program didn't work. I ask them, "Did you watch all the videos? Did you finish the book? Did you complete the activities?"

Their answer is always no.

Most people don't want to actually change their lives. They only want to confirm their preexisting belief that they're incapable of improving their lot in life. They want to defer responsibility for the unfortunate circumstances they're in.

For the people seeking that confirmation, there's

nothing I can do. I can't force you to sit in front of a computer and create a blog.

In order to change your life, you have to decide – are you a hero or a failure? Are you someone who blames other people for your lot in life, or are you someone who takes control and responsibility for your successes and failures?

The business models in this book work. I don't say this just because I teach them; I say this because I live them.

I'm just like the guy on the hair-loss commercials who was not only the president of the Hair Grow Society but also a member. In the same way, I don't just teach this stuff; it's what I actually do. My entire business is based on writing books, blogging, and podcasting.

If you commit right now to stick with these business models, you can be like all of my other successful followers.

Right now, you might have a little voice in the back of your mind that's feeding your doubts. "Oh, this will work for other people, but it won't work for me because I'm too old, I'm too young, I'm too smart, I'm too dumb, I'm too rich, I'm too poor."

All of that is a lie. It's just an excuse not to work hard, and it's not even a good excuse.

It doesn't matter what country you're from, what language you speak, or what your experience is. These business models work. You can become a hero simply by deciding to transform your life and follow these steps.

Keeping it simple is the critical part of this process. Here are three steps to help you along the way:

1. Set a simple financial goal.
2. Commit to spending a small amount of time on the process.

3. Consistent action leads to success.

It is the tortoise who wins, not the hare. It is easy to get excited about this book, spend twelve hours a day working on a project, and get burned out after a week. It's the person who blogs an hour a day every day for a year who experiences the big success.

If you slowly generate momentum, that momentum becomes unstoppable, and you'll have the power of a freight train.

If you've ever seen what happens when a rabbit and a freight train collide, the rabbit does not win. You can become that freight train. You can become that hero if you make a commitment to take consistent action.

26

THE COMMITMENT

Your final step is to make a commitment to me and, more importantly, yourself. Write this down and put it somewhere in your house where you can see it.

"I'm going to dedicate X many hours a week for X number of weeks to X project. My goal is to make X amount money."

An example could be, "I'm going to dedicate two hours a day for six months to building a blog that generates $100 a month in profit."

That's a small and achievable target. I want you to start there because, when you hit that goal after three weeks, you can move on to the next one.

By having a clear, written down goal and a commitment for the amount of time you'll invest in reaching that goal, the odds of your success skyrocket.

It's the people who don't take this tiny action step and write this down that become failures instead of heroes.

I want every person who reads this book to be a hero. I don't want to transform a dozen or even a thousand lives. I want to transform a million lives, and I want you to be part of that army of people whose lives I've transformed dramatically.

Make a commitment right now to a single business model. Sit down and say to yourself, "I'm going to stick with this and not be distracted by other advertisements, flashy programs, and business models until I get this dialed in. Until this one's making money, I'm not going to jump to the next one. I'm not going to quit, and I'm not going to try something else. I'm going to focus on one thing until I have success." If you make that commitment, success transforms from a possibility to an inevitability.

27

WHAT'S NEXT?

Your next step is to take action. Enter your email address by clicking the link below so that I can communicate with you and answer your questions.

I handle every single email personally. Every day, I get an email from someone who says, "Jonathan, I sent you an email to see if you'd actually reply." I always do.

I'm a real person. It's not my VA replying to people, and I don't have a page on my website that says, "I no longer answer emails." I'm a real person who wants to talk to you. When you see me as a real person, you'll be able to envision your life transforming into mine.

While I've carried the ball by writing this book, publishing it, and getting it into your hands, it's your turn to take action, and it could start with something as simple as communicating with me.

If you want more information, there are loads of additional training on my website for each of these sixteen business models. However, there's an even better way to learn more.

I have a Facebook group where a community of other people just like you are all connected to each other. They are each building their own business models, and they are always communicating, supporting, and helping each other to grow. If you join this group, they will welcome you into this community and support you in whichever endeavor you lock into.

Surrounding yourself with a group of people that are on the same journey will unlock everything you've ever hoped for.

It's often isolation that causes the independent entrepreneur to fail. Being by yourself, having those doubting voices, wondering if you're doing it wrong, and lacking the confirmation that you're not making a mistake is a scary place to be. That's not the life I want for you.

That's why I've built this community where you can connect with other people who are on the same journey as you.

Some of them are ahead of you, and, as you grow, new members will join and be behind you. You will become part of a consistent chain of people who are all tied to each other, climbing to the top of the mountain and achieving the same levels of success.

The final thing I want you to think about is how this book can help other people. I encourage you to tell other people about this book, share the message, and write positive reviews.

If you followed through on this process and found it to be a good experience, just writing a review will help ten or even one hundred other people find this book. That means more people will get the same help you found.

This is not a zero-sum game. There is enough money, treasure, and reward out there for everybody to share. Share your adventures, share your experience, and join me on this journey.

I can't wait to see you on the other side, where together we can create havoc and shout at the moon that we Serve No Master.

To JOIN the TRIBE and get access to a boatload of free training, just click this link.

https://ServeNoMaster.com/fire

28

MY GLORIOUS SOCCER CAREER

I wish I could tell you a story of glory and wonder as my soccer coach finally learned to believe in me. Unfortunately, my junior varsity coach demonstrated the very short-sightedness that kept him from coaching the varsity team.

In the first game with Doug and I as goalies, he let each of us play for one half of the game. Doug let four goals sail past his hands. Only one goal snuck past me. Statistically, Doug was four times worse than me.

But he was tall, so the coach kept giving him more time in the goal. He was baffled by our losing streak. While I wasn't the greatest goalie in the world, Doug always let more goals in than I did. The coach kept shortening my game time, and our team began losing by larger and larger margins.

Eventually, two of the regular players would stand in the goal to either side of Doug to try and make up for his inability to stop goals. It's not Doug's fault. He didn't want to be a goalie, and he probably doesn't even remember this story. The coach forced a player into a position he'd never played before because he was tall.

We never won another game after that.

Boy. I almost just ended this book on a real downer. There's no way I can let that happen. Remember that even though I didn't get to hoist the junior varsity soccer trophy over my shoulders, I did get to start my own business, move to a tropical island, marry my awesome wife and have three wonderful children.

It all started when I realized that nobody would believe in me, so I started believing in myself.

If you believe in yourself, it's time to get out of the stands and into the game. Let's make your dream into a reality. Are you ready to fire your boss?

ONE LAST CHANCE

You've made it to the end of the book. You even read my entire soccer story. Thanks!

As a special reward, I'm going to sweeten the pot. I really want us to be friends and turn this into a conversation.

Just enter your email address here:

ServeNoMaster.com/Fire

I'll give you a ton of FREE cool resources to kickstart your journey, including:

1. Quit Your Job Checklist

The "Ready to Retire" checklist that lets you know the exact moment you can fire your boss forever. Mark the moment on your calendar when you can start living a life of freedom.

2. Author and Entrepreneur Accelerator - Lifetime Membership

Get lifetime access to the most powerful group you will ever join. As a permanent member of my private accelerator, you will get free content daily as well as support from thousands of others on the same path.

Every day there are new training videos, stories of success and moments of inspiration...all waiting for you.

3. Five Day Business Challenge - Complimentary Ticket

Each month, I run a challenge with interviews from 25 experts at building an online business. Together we will refine your online dreams and help you focus on the best path for YOUR life. At the end of the challenge, you will know the exact steps to take to break the chains to a job you no longer love.

4. Get My Next Book Free

Members of my tribe get complimentary review and beta reader access to my new books before anyone else in the world knows. Get a chance to read my next book AND affect the final version with your suggestions and opinions.

You get these bonuses as well as a few surprises when you enter your best email address below.

Accelerate your success and click the link below to get instant access:

ServeNoMaster.com/Fire

THE DAY THE EARTH STOOD STILL

It was a couple of days after Christmas, and I'd put my entire life on the line. Months of work, years of preparation and strategy – and $7,000 of my family's money.

I'd invested it all – everything – on one wild idea that I hoped would save my sanity and give me financial freedom. And now the roulette wheel was spinning.

Two days earlier, the last of my credit cards was frozen. All of my bank accounts were empty. If the ball didn't land on my number, my life was about to come crashing down around my ears. It sounds like an incredible risk, but I knew that if I didn't do it, I'd go crazy.

What makes a regular guy so desperate?

For years I had been working as a "fixer" for small businesses, selling my time for dollars. Making videos, writing articles, working on code until late at night. If they needed it, I did it. I was a human drone!

I needed to escape that life and move to the next level. My clients had turned into my bosses, and I was desperate to extricate myself from the constant phone calls, emails, and texts that chased me every day.

Sitting in front of my computer that morning, all I had left was hope. If this didn't pay off, I would have to declare bankruptcy. And I didn't exactly have a supportive environment. Everyone around me told me I was a gullible idiot, that I was working on some get-rich-quick scheme, and that I was too lazy to do "real work." But there comes a moment in life when you just have to take that leap of faith and bet on yourself.

10 am, my first product went live – a digital training course explaining everything I did online and how to build a base of clients. Sure, I was sick of being a "local consultant," but I also knew there were tons of people who'd bend over backward to have what I had.

The first sale came in, and I was jumping up and down in my seat like a little kid, so nervous I wanted to throw up. One sale alone wasn't nearly enough to save me – I was almost ten grand in the hole. Each little sale sent me an alert to my phone as the email came in.

You made a sale!

I couldn't believe it. The pennies turned into dollars. The dollars turned into hundreds and then thousands. Was it possible? I could already start to taste success.

Within twenty-four hours, I had paid off all of my credit cards. They were way beyond "unfrozen." They were on fire. I was in the black, and the sales kept rolling in. My little idea turned into something beyond my wildest expectations. In twenty-four hours, there were over 1,700 sales. After paying off all my debts, over $10,000 in profit was sitting my PayPal account.

From negative 7,000 to plus 10,000 in a single weekend. I couldn't think of a better way to ring in the new year. I went up to Washington, DC to celebrate with one of my buddies. All night, my phone kept buzzing in my pocket. Sale after sale continued to rock in while I was rocking in the new year. I was making money faster than I was spending it for the first time in my life.

Even when I was asleep, money continued to pour into my account. And I'd gotten addicted to that little buzzing noise from my cell phone. I could barely nod off before it started up again. With a list of thousands of satisfied customers, my life changed forever. I would never have to drink energy drinks at 5 AM and "grind" at some gig ever again.

I was finally in control of my financial destiny, and I felt my first taste of real freedom.

How was I supposed to know it would get more complicated from there?

ARE YOU READY TO SERVE NO MASTER?

You've just read the first chapter from Serve No Master, the flagship book in the series and the official Book One. You can grab it for free on Kindle Unlimited right now ;)

Click Here to Grab Keep Reading

FOUND A TYPO?

While every effort goes into ensuring that this book is flawless, it is inevitable that a mistake or two will slip through the cracks.

If you find an error of any kind in this book, please let me know by visiting:

ServeNoMaster.com/typos

I appreciate you taking the time to notify me. This ensures that future readers never have to experience that awful typo. You are making the world a better place.

ABOUT THE AUTHOR

Born in Los Angeles, raised in Nashville, educated in London - Jonathan Green has spent years wandering the globe as his own boss - but it didn't come without a price. Like most people, he struggled through years of working in a vast, unfeeling bureaucracy.

And after the backstabbing and gossip of the university system threw him out of his job, he was "totally devastated" – stranded far away from home without a paycheck coming in. Despite having to hang on to survival with his finger-nails, he didn't just survive, he thrived.

In fact, today he says that getting fired with no safety net was the best thing that ever happened to him – despite the stress, it gave him an opportunity to rebuild and redesign his life.

One year after being on the edge of financial ruin, Jonathan had replaced his job, working as a six-figure SEO consultant. But with his rolodex overflowing with local businesses and their demands getting higher and higher, he knew that he had to take his hands off the wheel.

That's one of the big takeaways from his experience. Lifestyle design can't just be about a job replacing income, because often, you're replicating the stress and misery that comes with that lifestyle too!

Thanks to smart planning and personal discipline, he started from scratch again – with a focus on repeatable, passive income that created lifestyle freedom.

He was more successful than he could have possibly expected. He traveled the world, helped friends and family, and moved to an island in the South Pacific.

Now, he's devoted himself to breaking down every hurdle entrepreneurs face at every stage of their development, from developing mental strength and resilience in the depths of depression and anxiety, to developing financial and business literacy, to building a concrete plan to escape the 9-to-5, all the way down to the nitty-gritty details of teaching what you need to build a business of your own.

In a digital world packed with "experts," there are few people with the experience to tell you how things really work, why they work, and what's actually working in the online business world right now.

Jonathan doesn't just have the experience, he has it in a variety of spaces. A best-selling author, a "Ghostwriter to the Gurus" who commands sky-high rates due to his ability to deliver captivating work in a hurry, and a video producer who helps small businesses share their skills with their communities.

He's also the founder of the Serve No Master podcast, a weekly show that's focused on financial independence, networking with the world's most influential people, writing epic stuff online, and traveling the world for cheap.

All together, it makes him one of the most captivating and accomplished people in the lifestyle design world, sharing the best of what he knows with total transparency, as part of a mission to free regular people from the 9-to-5 and live on their own terms.

Learn from his successes and failures and Serve No Master.

Find out more about Jonathan at:
ServeNoMaster.com

BOOKS BY JONATHAN GREEN

Non-Fiction

Serve No Master Series

Serve No Master

Breaking Orbit

20K a Day

Control Your Fate

Breakthrough (coming soon)

Habit of Success Series

PROCRASTINATION

Influence and Persuasion

Overcome Depression

Stop Worrying and Anxiety

Love Yourself

Conquer Stress

Law of Attraction

Mindfulness and Meditation Ultimate Guide

Meditation Techniques for Beginners

I'm Not Shy

Coloring Depression Away with Adult Coloring Books

Don't be Quiet

How to Make Anyone Like You

Develop Good Habits with S.J. Scott

How to Quit Your Smoking Habit

The Weight Loss Habit

Seven Secrets

Seven Networking Secrets for Jobseekers

Biographies

The Fate of my Father

Complex Adult Coloring Books

The Dinosaur Adult Coloring Book

The Dog Adult Coloring Book

The Celtic Adult Coloring Book

The Outer Space Adult Coloring Book

The 2nd Celtic Adult Coloring Book

Irreverent Coloring Books

Dragons Are Bastards

Fiction

Gunpowder and Magic

The Outlier (As Drake Blackstone)

ONE LAST THING

Reviews are the lifeblood of any book on Amazon and especially for the independent author. If you would click five stars on your Kindle device or visit this special link at your convenience, that will ensure that I can continue to produce more books. A quick rating or review helps me to support my family, and I deeply appreciate it.

Without stars and reviews, you would never have found this book. Please take just thirty seconds of your time to support an independent author by leaving a rating.

Thank you so much!

To leave a review go to ->

https://servenomaster.com/firereview

Sincerely,

Jonathan Green

ServeNoMaster.com

NOTES

2. Unlock Your Superpower

1. http://www.usfinancialcapability.org/downloads/NFCS_2015_Report_-Natl_Findings.pdf.